Thrifting
for
Cash

An Inexpensive Way to Build a Part-time Home-based Business with Little Money Out-of-Pocket and Earn BIG Profits

IOLA YHAP

Table of Contents

Introduction

I want to thank you and congratulate you for downloading this book, Thrifting For Cash: An Inexpensive Way to Build A Part-Time Home-Based Business with Little Money Out Of Pocket and Earn BIG Profits (A Beginner's Guide to Making Extra Money Thrifting). My name is Iola Yhap and Thrifting for Cash is one of my part-time businesses. My gift to you for purchasing this book, is a FREE list of _101 Brands to Get When Thrifting_[1]. Don't procrastinate because of fear, take the list with you to help yourself get started.

The tips and strategies I discuss in this book are things that I've practiced and implemented in my thrifting business. This business has allowed me to pay off debts and helped me to invest in myself and my education. Through income from thrifting I was able to pay for classes, books, coaching, equipment etc to further my education and career. These are things that I otherwise would not have been able to do if I didn't "Thrift for Cash". If you are an experienced thrifter who uses thrifting as a business, this book may not be for you. This book was written for those who have never been thrifting before,

---

1   http://eepurl.com/LOFdD

those you have never thought or thrifting as a business, or those who have never used thrifting as a business. In this book you will find proven simple steps and strategies that I have used to shop at thrift stores, consignment shops, tag/garage/yard sales, estate sales and flea markets with little or no money out of pocket and resell the items for 50% or more profit.

Whether you have a full time or part time job, unemployed or under employed, you too can thrift to create income. We do live in an age where our jobs are no longer guaranteed, the word pension is almost unheard of in most jobs. The sense of job security is no longer that way it was. Sadly, we live in an age where there are no jobs, an age where we take out student loans for higher education, graduate but cannot find a job or have a job that has nothing to do with our field of study. Many of us never have or will never see a return on our educational investment. As a result people are seeking creative ways to bring some kind of security in their lives. Be one of those people who think outside of the box, since you are reading this book I know that you are one of those people seeking ways to build a business that does not require a lot of money.

Many of us live in areas where there are thrift stores, whether it's non-profit community thrift stores run by churches or other small non-profit organizations or nationally known thrift stores such as Savers, Salvation Army and Goodwill. If you live in an area that does not have these stores, you can also take advantage of local residents who have used and sometimes new items at their yard sale or estate sale. Take advantage of yourself, look around your home, your closet for items that you no longer want and sell them for a profit. It is that easy to start. However, to continue you will need drive, motivation, tenacity, consistency, persistence and discipline. To be successful in this business all depends on you.

Anyone can thrift for cash. Thrifters or Pickers as they are sometimes called range in age and social backgrounds such as, college students, high school students, employees, non-employees, and business owners just to name a few. Thrifting is a great way to help pay off debts, pay for education, take vacations, create a savings account etc. Some of you may feel scared or overwhelmed about the idea of going to Thrift Stores, Consignments Shops, Estate Sales etc.

In the chapters to come you will learn how simple thrifting for cash really is. Imagine making an extra $200, $500, $2000 per month? Thrifting is a way for you to create that extra income for yourself. In the chapters to come you will learn simple and what may seem like common sense ways to make money thrifting. However these are simple steps that people often miss or don't practice when using thrifting as a business. I encourage you to highlight and take notes. Dedicate time to perform some of the simple yet essential tasks I speak about. Now grab that pen and paper and let's get started.

CHAPTER 01
Thrifting Basics

What is Thrifting?

Thrifting is a frugal practice to recycle and reuse items for any specific purpose. In this book the purpose for thrifting will be to make money.

People who usually thrift for income are called Pickers. This is because they go to thrift stores, estate sales, yard sales, flea markets, consignment shops, auctions, online markets and "pick" through items that they believe they can sell online as well as offline to make a profit and produce income for themselves. Pickers range in various age groups and backgrounds. Thrifting for cash is a great way to teach inexperienced entrepreneurs how to start and run a successful part-time business, as well as help existing entrepreneurs to have an additional way to make money. As mentioned in the title, this business is one of the few that is flexible and requires very little money out of pocket. Now that you have the concept of what thrifting is, let's learn how to do it and make money.

CHAPTER 02

Seven Simple Tips to Become Successful Thrifter

Treat Thrifting like its business- Set specific days and time frames to go thrifting. I have a whiteboard in my home with my schedule for going thrifting for the week. It is important to write things down. Not only will you be writing them down to remember them but you will be writing them down to keep focused, stay on track and hold yourself accountable to complete whatever tasks you have written for yourself. You can choose to have a whiteboard like me, or you can choose something else an online calendar, notebook etc. Whatever method you choose, just do it. There is power in writing things down.

Be Consistent- Consistency creates a sense of accomplishment or seriousness. Being consistent gives you something to look forward to and helps you to stay motivated and persistent. Consistency creates a sense of importance. Your thrifting business is important. Remember it can be your ticket towards extra money to pay bills, invest, save, make a living ... whatever you choose for it to be then it can be that.

Stay committed- stick to the days and times you set for thrifting, treat it like it is your job, your business... because it is. Think about it for a second...at your regular job (whether you have one or had one) you are expected to show up every day, or specific days at specific times. Your thrifting business should be no different. Respect your business, show up for it at the times you have scheduled. This is why writing your schedule down and looking at it is extremely important for the success of your thrifting business. Be accountable for yourself.

Find a niche- especially in the beginning thrift for things that you love or are most knowledgeable about. For example if you like fashion, then thrift for clothes, look for brands that you know are high quality and will sell. Picking something you love will make your thrifting business exciting, thus easy to accomplish. Now as you become more experienced, venturing out into other niches can become exciting as well.

Educate Yourself- There is no price on education and in this day and age there are many free ways to educate yourself for free or with little money out of pocket. The internet is one of the most powerful tools known to man. You have to make it work for you. Make sure you research items that you are interested in selling. For example certain brands of clothing sell for more money or sell faster than others. Research how to offer great customer service because this is an essential part in thrifting for cash. Research places that you will be interested in selling your items. "Research research research" in thrifting is like "location location location" in real estate, it's everything. Set specific times to do this in your business. I have learned a plethora of things from the internet. Google and Youtube should be your best friends when it comes to research. I can honestly say that I've learned more from these two places than from going to college and earning 2 degrees, one of which includes a Masters degree...It is the honest truth. This is how powerful the internet is, it has answers to questions at your fingertips. So take advantage of the internet, use it to work for you and your education, your success.

Think outside the Box- Think of items that others may shy away from or not pay attention to and invest in those items. I say to do this because often times there is very little or less competition when you do so. Some of us are programmed to get things we are familiar with or things we like. When we go shopping for the most part we go to the section that have our size. Shopping to make money is different. For example, I am a woman and I sell mostly clothing but I focus mostly on men's large sizes because there is less competition in this area than in other areas of clothing. A jeans or shirt that is a 5x will sell much faster and for more money that a smaller size. The same goes of shoes and other articles of clothing, look for the biggest sizes. Big sizes usually equal big money for you.

Be friendly to your managers and cashiers- This may seem like common sense but trust me, a lot of people do not practice this. They believe that they are paying their money therefore they can do whatever they want...WRONG. Write this down in your notes "Cashiers can make or break your thrifting experience." Keep in mind as a result they can make or break your profit margin. Remember why you are in this business or why you want to be in this business... it's to make money. So do not let someone else interfere with your money because of your actions toward them. Let's keep in mind that people do business with those they know, like and trust. If the cashiers don't feel any of those attributes toward to then you are missing out big time. If the cashiers or managers know you, like you and trust you then it's almost guaranteed that they will treat you well. I've had countless occasions where cashiers have given me items for deep discounts or even free because of my demeanor and the way I approach them. This has not only happened in stores but at yard sales too. A worker at the thrift store may alert you about certain items that they are expecting or specific items that are not on the floor yet that you may be interested in. They will go out of their way to take 'care" of you all because you have the correct attitude towards them. Remember some thrift stores are not the best places to shop or work in so kindness and friendliness goes a mighty long way. So remember to be courteous, and be curious. Curiosity can bring you great bargains at deeply discounted prices and help you to make lots of money. Ask questions.

CHAPTER 03

Popular Items to Thrift for on a Budget

Knowing what items to sell is essential in making sure that the turnovers for the items are as quick as possible. Don't be afraid to list winter clothes in July or summer clothes in December because if selling internationally, someone's winter may be your summer and vice versa. Here are some popular Items To thrift For on A Budget

Clothes, shoes, bags- Jeans, Men's Shirts, Winter Jackets usually sell very well online. Especially if selling internationally as well as domestically. A lot of countries outside of the United States love US brands of clothing. Again, large sizes usually sell faster because there is less competition.

Coffee mugs- Coffee Mugs is a niche that can be successful. Most people who buy these are collectors. Popular brands such Disney and Hallmark usually sells very well. There are other popular brands as well that you can research or you can get my free list _101 Brands to Get when Thrifting_[1]. You can make a good profit on coffee mugs since often times they can be purchased for less than $2 and resell from $9.99 and upwards. Let's write a scenario down and look at the math for a quick second.

You purchase 5 coffee mugs for $2.00 each (I've never paid more than $2.00) this equals $10.00

Let's say you've sold all of the mugs for $10.00 (minimum of what's I've sold for)

$10 spent out of pocket

$10*5 = $50 worth of sold items

$40 profit (you've made to put towards whatever you "why" is).

Now imagine selling 10 or 20 mugs ... watch your profit margin increase!!!

Books- Although there are many electronic book readers, traditional books are still in demand. Textbooks for certain subjects such as math and science usually sell very well. Books about unique topics also sell well. For example a book about vintage cars will sell much faster and for more money than books about basketball simply because vintage cars are a rare topic. You can find books at various places. Some areas some- times have book sales. Places such as libraries have several book sales per year. Last year I bought tons of books from a church sale. Religious books usually sell well. You can also find books at garage sales, estate sales and thrift stores. Look out for 1st edition books, or books that are a part of a series. Usually people go looking for the ones missing from their series and some are willing to pay a good amount of money for

1   http://eepurl.com/LOFdD

it too. Stay away from books that are in poor condition such as falling apart or have lots of highlights and underlines in them. Books are great items to sell on Amazon. Books are one of those thrifted items that can bring a very large profit margin. I usually pay $1 for my books and I sell them anywhere from $15.00 - $97.00. Do the math for the profit you can achieve from selling books. Remember you are not spending a lot out of pocket for these items.

Games (board and video) - Games are very popular. Older games are usually high in demand. If you do buy board games, make sure they have all of the pieces in them. This is usually a challenge if a game has a lot of pieces. If a piece is missing, sometimes you can buy that piece online, usually on ebay or you can even contact the manufacturer of the game to see if they have the piece. They may even send it to you for free. Video games for old consoles such as Nintendo and Sega Genesis are sought after; and as a result provides descent profit margins. Consoles themselves are hot items to sell. Many times they do not have to be in working condition to sell them. You just make sure that you disclose that in your description when selling the item.

Electronics- Electronics and electronic parts are often times in demand especially if a specific item is discontinued. Sometimes it's better to sell an electronic item in parts for a higher profit margin. For example you can sell parts of a camera (lens etc) for more money rather than selling the entire camera. The same can be done for items such as older blenders, vacuum cleaners etc. When it comes to electronics don't discriminate. There is someone out there who is looking for a part to an old electronic item they have and they are sometimes willing to pay a hefty amount of money for it.

Stuffed Animals- Ebay has listed stuff animals as one of the most popular items to sell online. It doesn't matter if they are new or used, these stuffed animals can be sold from 9.99 and upwards. Cartoon characters from Disney are popular items to sell. Vintage characters usually sell for a higher profit margin. Pickers sometimes sell stuffed animals in a group or a lot (as they are usually called) to make more money. Look out for stuffed animals or characters that are old and are no longer "active". Some examples are characters from old Disney movies. Once I found stuffed animals for the Three Stooges in their black and white striped outfits.

Toys- Toys are good to sell especially during the Christmas season. Popular toys and collectibles sell incredibly fast online as well as offline, although it is better to sell popular items online to get a bigger range of customers. Like other categories, older toys will usually bring a higher profit margin. Toys can be sold new or used on most online market places. On Amazon however a used toys should be listed as "collectible" instead of used. Any toys for babies must be brand new in order to sell on Amazon. Make sure you look up market places policies before you list an item to sell. The policies are usually found on the company's website.

CDs, DVDs, Tapes, VHS- These items sell well, especially online. VHS will sell for more money if they are new in the shrink wrap. Many Pickers lot or put these items in a group to get the most profit. These items can usually be found for under $2.00 at thrift store, yard sales and estate sales.

Memorabilia- Different memorabilia are great items to sell. These can include sports, television, or movie memorabilia. Make sure that these items are in great condition to be able to sell them for high profit.

Artwork- Art can transcend cultural differences and as a result they can sell for a lot of money. It doesn't matter if the painting is done by a popular artist or not. Beauty is based on one's perspective and the online community can offer a wide range of market for it. Usually if I'm unsure of the price for an artwork I would list it as an auction and have buyers bid online. You don't have to be an expert to pick artwork. Since you are a beginner, look for unusual and unique pieces of artwork.

CHAPTER 04
Where to Sell Your Items

Y ou can sell your thrifted items online or offline. Online market places are constantly changing to efficiently tend to customers' needs. To help you be aware of some of the market places available, I've listed some popular ones below with a little background on each. There are other sites and apps not listed below so do you research to find other platforms for your Thrifted business. For more in-depth information, you can visit the companies' websites.

Online Market Places

Ebay

Ebay is widely known as "The world's Marketplace", it was founded in 1995. I see Ebay as an online flea market and one stop shop where you can buy and sell anything from around the world. According to Ebay's website Ebay has more than

124 million active users all around the world, and more than 500 million items are listed in this platform. They provide a platform where sellers big and small can compete and win. Ebay also is a platform where buyers and sellers connect. This marketplace is ever evolving, they now have a delivery service where certain items are delivered to customers door within hours of ordering from their website. Ebay gladly welcomes new used items; even items that do not work such as electronics just make sure you disclose if an item does not work and that you are selling the item "as is" in your description).

Amazon

According to Amazon's website prides itself "to be Earth's most customer-centric company, where customers can find and discover anything they might want to buy online, and endeavors to offer its customers the lowest possible prices." Amazon prides itself in being the world's largest online marketplace. No more are the days where Amazon is just for books. Today you can shop for your livelihood on Amazon. Amazon welcomes new, used and collectible items. However they are accept as used or collectible. For example anything for a baby must be brand new in order to sell it on amazon. On the other hand you can sell books and other items as used or collectible. Collectible meaning in "like new" condition or the 1st edition of something. Amazon however is well known for offering new items. Here is a list of categories that you can find on Amazon:

Books	Movies	Music
Games	Digital Downloads	Electronics & Computers
Home & Garden	Toys	Kids & Baby

Grocery   Apparel   Shoes & Jewelry

Health & Beauty   Sports & Outdoor   Tools

Auto & Industrial

Amazon has Fulfillment Centers accross the globe,. This enables Amazon to provide fast, reliable shipping directly from Amazon's retail sites. Their Customer Service Center provide 24/7 support to buyers. Those who sell on Amazon can either be individual merchants (where sellers process and ship orders themselves) or Fullfillment by Amazon sellers also known FBA. FBA where sellers' merchandise are sold and shipped by Amazon. As of the date this book was written it cost $40 monthly to be a FBA Seller. There are perks for being a FBA seller. Some of which includes:

Having someone else run your business for you and take care of the customer service aspect. You have to label and ship merchandise to an Amazon fulfillment center and they take care of the rest.

Merchandise qualifies for Amazon Prime where Prime members will receive FREE shipping as well as receive their item in 2 days.

Fba items are marked with the "Fullfillment by Amazon" logo which provide buyers with the assurance that their shopping experience is handled by Amazon, This includes packing, shipping and returns (if necessary) Since trust is extremely important when shopping online, merchandise with the FBA logo are more likely to have increased sales.

Craigslist

Craigslist is Local classifieds and forums website that is community moderated, and free. According to craigslist , "more than 60 million million people in the US alone uses craiglslist monthly and the site receives over 80 million ads each month. Craigslist is found in USA, Canada, Europe, Asia/Pacific/Middle,East,Oceciana,Latin Amercia and Africa. Some categories in craigslist includes:

Foe Sale	Jobs	Housing
Goods	Services	Romance
Gigs	Local Activities	Advice

Poshmark

Poshmark is an application currently used for apple and android devices. You simply download the app and create your own closet/"store". You can sell new and used items on Poshmark, mainly fashion. You can also trade on Poshmark. If you like something in someone else's closet you can either buy it or offer to trade for one of your items. New as well as used items are sold on this platform.

Poshmark has an event known as "Posh Parties". Posh parties are virtual buying and selling parties that happen in the actual Poshmark app. Sellers and buyers can browse, buy, and even list items together with friends. Popular listing and shopping party themes often include, Designer Handbags & Shoes and Cocktail Dresses. Poshmark also has designer themed parties where brands such as Chanel, Louis Vuitton, Coach, and Michael Kors are often featured. One thing that I love about Poshmark is that sellers can create an entire look to show potential buyers how they can put together a particular look based on one or more items being offered for sale. For example, a buyer may be selling a leopard top but will pair the top with a red pleated skirt, white shoes, pearl earrings and a red bag. This visual helps potential buyers to envision the various outfits they can create if they should buy the top.

Etsy

Etsy is an e-commerce website focused on handmade or vintage items, as well as art and craft supplies. DIYers (Do it yourself) use Etsy as their to go place to sell products and items they've made. You can get more information at *www.etsy.com*. Some categories in Etsy includes:

Photography	Art	Clothing
Food Products	Jewelery	Bath & Beauty
Bedding	Toys	Furniture
Electronics	Kitchenwares	Home Decor

Facebook

At the time is book is written Facebook is the #1 Social Media Site. According to Facebook its mission is to "give people the power to share and make the world more open and connected". Below Facebook has listed some unique about using Facebook for business.

"Discoverable: When people search for you on Facebook, they'll be able to find you.

Connected: Have one-on-one conversations with your customers, who can like your Page, read your posts and share them with friends, and check in when they visit.

Timely: Your Page can help you reach large groups of people frequently, with messages tailored to their needs and interests.

Insightful: Analytics on your Page will give you a deeper understanding of your customers and your marketing activities.

When you set up your Page, you can request a web address like *facebook.com/yourgreatcompany*, which makes it easy to find. To maximize the impact, include this address on your business card, website and other marketing materials.

Your Page is an extension of your business. It's an easy way to share updates and more with the people who matter most. It's ready to help you engage your customers on desktop and on mobile."

Facebook can be an avenue for selling a variety of items from furniture to books. The good thing about Facebook is that it makes it so easy to share and publish photos of items to family, friends and customers. For more information about using Facebook for business please visit *Facebook.com*

Pinterest

Pinterest Online scrapbooking platform isn't just for DIYers anymore. According to consumer insight firm Semiocast, Pinterest has more than 70 million users. Many experts have predicted that having Pinterest for business will supercede Facebook and other social media sites. Pinterest is a great platform for selling items not only because it's very visual but it is also an app. More and more people are using their cell phones for shopping, so shopping through an app like Pinterest is very convenient and efficient. You can use Pinterest not only to list yours items but do upload videos or presentations you may have about your Thrifting business. Pinterest can be used to tell a story about your business, remember that people love stories. I recently paid a sale price of $100 for a course about Pinterest for business. I believe that the course is originally almost to $300. This price should give you an idea about the direction Pinterest for Business is going. Below are five reasons outlined by entrepreneur.com about why you should use Pinterest for business.

"No. 1: Make your website Pin-friendly.

Users can "pin" items to their personal boards by using a downloadable "Pin It" widget. To encourage consumers to engage with your company's content...

No. 2: Organize your content.

Pinterest enables all users to create themed boards...businesses should organize content by theme, making it easier for other users to find and browse content.

"If you're a home décor shop, organize boards so you have a home accessories board, a couches and chairs board and a pillows board...

No. 3: Brand your pins.

While it takes more time, the experts agree that branding the photos that are uploaded to Pinterest is worth the added effort.

No. 4: Include shopper-friendly information.

Compared to other social sites like Facebook or Twitter ... Pinterest users approach the platform with a shopping mindset.

No. 5: Engage the community.

Aside from uploading new photos of inventory, the experts say business owners should seek to become active in the online

community." Experts also advise to include logo on pictures.
www.Entrepreneur.com

Offline Market Places
Flea markets

A flea market or a 'swap meet" as it is sometimes called is an arena that rents space to people who want to sell or barter merchandise. At the flea markets bargaining is expected. Vendors sell used and new items. Flea markets often as food, clothing, bedding, books, electronics, household items, kitchenware, tools, art, artifacts and the list goes on. Flea markets can be held annually or semiannually, monthly, weekends or every day. Vendors usually have tents and tables set up or even set up their merchandise on the floor/road etc. Flea markets provide great exposure for sellers and their merchandise. The flea market set up also gives the seller a chance to interact face to face with buyers from around the country. Niche items usually sell very well at flea markets.

Consignments Stores/Shops

You can buy items inexpensively at thrift stores then take them to a consignment store in your area and have them sell it for you. They usually sell it at a higher price that what you paid at the thrift stores. Once the item is sold you split the sale with the consignment store. Some stores also give you credit to use in their store if your item sells. High end name brand items or very rare pieces works best for consignment stores/shops.

Antique booths- Some areas have thrift malls where you can rent a booth and set up your items. Some malls charge a fee in addition to rent and take a percentage of your items that sell. Antique booths are great for rare, unique or big items such as home décor, furniture etc. At some Antique malls the seller does not have to physically be there to sell items, the mall sells the items for the seller. The items are priced/coded and employees of the mall "checks out" the items. Various antique booth malls disperse sellers' payments at varying times of the month so this is something that will be included in the contract if you do decide to own an antique booth.

Niche Boutiques- some boutiques look for specific items to resell. I have a friend who owns a vintage boutique in town. I take some my items to her and she consigns them for me. She provides the advertisement and storage and whenever she sells any of my items we split an agreed percentage of the sale. I encourage you to research niche boutiques in your area and see if you can partner with them.

Family and Friends- sell items to people you know and love. I buy thrifted vintage clothing and sell them to my loved ones as well as co-workers. I have specific days or set appointments where people can come to my home and try on pieces. I sometimes provide a light snack and have a "girl's night" selling my thrifted finds and bonding with the ladies. You can choose to sell to your loved ones however you want, the possibilities are endless.

Yard sale- It's a good idea to hold a yard sale when you're trying to make room for more merchandise. Try to price the items reasonably and be open to negotiation. The only expense for holding out a yard sale is advertisement expense. For the most part you do not have to spend money of advertisement. A marker and poster board usually does the trick. Yard sale does require your time and organization skills. The more organized your sale is people are more likely to stick around and shop.

Now that you know some of the basics grab your _101 Brands To Get When Thrifting List and let's go Thrifting!!!_[1]

---

1   http://eepurl.com/LOFdD

CHAPTER 05

Simple Ways to Make Your Thrifted Business Thrive

N ow you may think that these tips are common sense (which they are) but a lot of sellers don't follow them. As a result sellers get returns and bad reviews which equals to lost of money and a bad reputation. These two are definitely not a good combination. According to marketing experts such a Jim Cockrum, bad reviews can linger in the internet for years to come. So please beware of how important it is to please your customers. Below are some tips to help you gain positive reasons and little to no returns.

Presentation- Clean items before you take pictures or sell them to people. Cleaning can sometimes mean a simple wash in the washing machine, wiping something with a damp cloth or even dusting an item. Always make sure your items are presentable for your buyers. You do not need to spend a lot of money taking items to the cleaners. Take pictures of your items in well-lit areas. Most items sell very well if the pictures look good. Try to capture items in natural light or against a white background. Presentation does not need to be expensive, remember our goal is to spend little money out of pocket as possible.

The items below were taken on a chair covered with a white sheet against a white wall.

Be truthful with your listing- if there is a flaw with your item, please disclose it. You can do this by taking pictures of the flaw and in addition, put it in writing in your description when you list your item. For example if you are selling a mug and it has a chip, please take pictures of the chip and disclose it in the description. Pointing out flaws gives you credibility as a seller and helps you to gain new and repeat customers.

Another aspect where you must be truthful in your listing is shipping times. If you offer same or next business day shipping, please honor this and ship same or next business day. Try to ship items within 2 business days even if you don't disclose this. Customers love when they unexpectedly receive their items quickly. By shipping promptly customers are mostly likely to leave a good review and buy from you again. Both of these equal more money for your business.

Always seek ways to satisfy your customers- If your customer complains about your product, please don't argue with them. If they want a refund it is best to refund the money. It's better to lose a few dollars over one item than to lose a lot of money in the future because that customer does not return to buy from you, does not recommend you to others or even worst, write you a bad review. If you sold the item online and you feel like you're being scammed, contact the online marketplace and let them investigate. Your goal should be to keep moving and seek ways to continue to make more money. If the customer wants to return something and it's your fault, you must offer to pay the shipping for the returned item. A customer who was dissatisfied with an item once can be a repeat customer. This is only happen if you've handled the situation correctly. The "old" saying "the customer is always right" do still hold truth today. As a matter of fact it holds more true today in the information age than it did in the previous age. Remember bad reviews can follow your business for years, so you need to do your very best to avoid getting them. If you do get a bad review, go out of your way to prove to the customer that they are important and that you are willing to do something to rectify the situation.

Another way to satisfy your customer is to go the extra mile and offer free shipping. I usually offer free shipping if I know that I will make a big profit from the item. People love free shipping.

Send a smile to your customer- offer something for a discount or for free. It can be something as simple as a handwritten note, a card, or a pair of earrings. (I've included a pair of earrings I bought for $1.00 with an outfit I've sold because I believed that that earring looked nice with the outfit I sold). Anything handwritten is almost always appreciated. If I sell books, I usually included a free bookmark. You can find a pack of them at the dollar store. I want you to write down three ways (other than what I've listed) how you can send a smile to your customer. Now that you've written them down TAKE ACTION, implement them into your business.

Don't be afraid to ask for feedback- First let the customer know that if there is a problem with their purchase to contact you and that you will be more than happy to fix the problem. This usually prevents the customer from writing a bad review about you thus affecting your rating, if the item was sold online. You can ask the customer to rate your store if they are satisfied with their purchase and experience with you. Remember you just don't want customers, you want repeat customers. Repeat customers mean repeat money for you. Also if someone is satisfied doing business with you they will tell not just one person...remember this is the information age with the internet, they can tell hundreds and thousands of people about their experience with you. They can do this on several review sites including the site they bought your product from as well as Blogs, Facebook, Instagram, Twitter, Pinterest and all the other social media sites out there. These days word spread in the blink of an eye, it's up to you to make the word about your business a good one.

CHAPTER 06
Simple Steps to Save More Money Thrifting

Google thrift stores in your area. Call the stores to see if they have discount days, some stores even have loyalty cards which gives you a percentage off your purchases just for using your loyalty card. Some thrift stores have ½ off days for certain color price tags. Items, especially clothes are usually tagged with various colors such as pink, green, blue and yellow indicating that they are at a discounted price. Some thrift stores also have discounts for veterans and seniors, even students.

Find out if your thrift store has 'fill a bag day". Most stores provide a bag and you can pack as much items as your bag can hold and then pay a specific price. This is usually if not always an excellent way to make huge profit on items. Imagine filling you bag with 30 pieces of clothing and only pay $15.00, that's $2.00 per item. If you sell all of the items for only $15.00 you will earn $450.00 just by investing $15.00 cash and some of your time.

Some thrift stores as well as consignment stores have $1.00 day. This is where specific items are set up in one area and only cost $1.00 per item. Think of the huge profits you can make off of your $1.00 items.

I always go to the thrift stores on ½ off days and I only buy name brand items. I purchase mostly clothing but I do buy games, especially if they are still shrink wrapped, toys, dvds, cds, vhs(shrink wrapped) books and other odds and ends. The most I would pay for one article of clothing is $6.00 and the least I would list it online for resale is 14.99.

Estate sales and yard sales can also have great bargains. Most of the time the best items are sold in the beginning of the sale, however if you stick around long enough you can get deeply discounted and even free items from the sellers.

Remember we look for rare or brand name items to make a decent profit

CHAPTER 07
Things to keep in Mind

Not all thrift stores are the same

Thrift stores are just like other stores in town. Some of them have poor ventilation and lighting while others are set up in a good place with reasonable prices. Not all thrift stores are created equal. Just remember that for every thrift store out there may be several great pieces waiting to be discovered and make you money.

Visit all kinds of thrift stores

Many people have the wrong impression that the best merchandise comes from the well-to-do areas in town. A thrift buyer should never neglect going in middle or low class areas to scour for hidden treasures.

Sometimes thrift stores get their items from one supplier so there is a good chance that the merchandise received by the thrift store in an upscale area is the same kind items being brought to rural areas.

Make a list and go thrifting often

Walking into a thrift shop without any idea what to buy can lead being overwhelmed and going over budget. Create a list of specific items that are in demand for buyers. In addition, try to go as often as possible to have better chances of spotting great deals.

Be ready to dig

Shopping at thrift stores would require more effort on the buyer compared to retail stores because most items have already been picked out. This means that digging through a few layers is required to find something that no one has seen yet.

Carry cash

Thrift stores and yard sales will require cash payment so buyers should be prepared with it.

Dress appropriately

Thrifting means a whole day of running in and out of stores and digging through old and sometimes dusty items. Wear clothing that is comfortable and clothing you would not mind getting dirty.

Create a budget

Know exactly how much each item is worth so that it will be easier to establish a budget for it. Try to stick to the budget.

Ask for it

It is acceptable to haggle at thrift stores. Do not be afraid to ask for lower prices but if the price is still unreasonable after negotiations it is better to just walk away. Thrifters want to get a great deal just as much vendors want great profit.

Go early

The best deals are found at the start of the sale. It is true that items will be much cheaper towards the end of the sale but it is most likely that all the good things are gone.

Don't judge

Take a second look at seemingly unattractive items. Sometimes just a coat of paint for a piece of furniture or new buttons on a sweater can instantly transform the item. However, there is a fine line between minor adjustments and major overhauls. Leave things that are beyond repair or will take up too much of your time and money.

CHAPTER 08

Basic Tools to have for Thrifting

Tape measure- depending on what you are going to resell you may need a tape measure

Envelops- you will need various sizes envelops to ship your items.

Boxes- you should have various sizes boxes as well. You do not need to go out and spend money on boxes. Simply visit your local store and ask them for empty boxes, most of the stores throw these away.

Packing materials- you can get items such as bubble wraps and foam for free from your local store.

Computer/Phone- if you choose to sell online you will need a computer or a descent phone to take and upload pictures.

Printer- you will need a printer to print your stamps and packing slips if you choose to sell online. You will also need ink for your printer.

A Scale- having a scale is a must have for selling online because you need to weigh your packages for shipment. Digital scales are best.

Camera– remember pictures tell stories, make sure the stories about your thrifted items are good ones. (please don't buy anything expensive starting out).

Dress Form (if you sell clothing)- you can find dress forms inexpensively at thrift stores, department stores or online. Dress forms can make your clothing presentations look very professional.

Conclusion

Thank you again for purchasing this book!

I hope this book was able to help you learn how to create a part-time home-based business where you can make some extra money or use it as a way to create full-time income for you and your family.

The next step is to research places in your area and TAKE ACTION

Finally, if you enjoyed this book, please take the time to share your thoughts and post a review on Amazon. It'd be greatly appreciated. I want to you succeed in this business. Remember to get your free list below of _101 brands To Get When Thrifting_[1], copy it and take it with you.

Thank you and Go Thrifting!

---

1 http://eepurl.com/LOFdD

Resources

101 BRANDS YOU SHOULD LOOK OUT FOR WHEN THRIFTING
FOR CASH

Shirts/Blazers

Bionie
Southern Tide
Vineyard Vines
Fred Perry
Johnson Wollen Mills
Paul and Shark Yachting
Bugachi Umo
English Laundry
Greg Norman
High Noon
Lacoste
Ibiza
Tommy Bahama
Versace/istante
Robert Graham
HbarC

California Ranchwear
Joseph and Feiss
Rail Riders
Patagonia
Pendleton
Brooks Brothers
Ralph Lauren
Faconnable
Rivergold Western

Sweaters

Johnston of Elgin
Iceberg History
Marc Jacobs
Coogi
Bogner
Rugged Outdoor

Eddie Bauer

Final Home

Ermenegildo Zegna

Davis and Squire

Harley Davidson

Campus

Bape

LL Bean

Moffat Woollens

Agnes B

Alexander Wang

Jeans

G-Star

Big Star

Rock Revival

Frankie B

Husdon

Cofh

Nudie

Seven for All Mankind

Joes

Citizens of Humanity

Footwear

Noat

Todd's

Bally

Boc

Sas

Born

Via Spiga

Sperry

Bruno Magli

Ferragamos

Dansk

Mephisto

Santoni

Birkenstock

Sas Tripad

Fossil

Johnston& Murphy

Florsheim

Toms

Josef Siebel

Tony Lama

Sanita

Kate spade

Sesto Meucci

Keen

Ed hardy

Stuart Weitzman

Talbots

Donald J Pilner

Loints

Tsonga

Ariat

Charles David

Helle

Boden

Elizabeth Stuart

St. John
Casual Corner
Waldlaufer
Dexter

Baseball Gloves

Rawlins
Muzino
Easton
Wilson
Macgror
Addidas

Outerwear

Sierra Designs...jackets
Alpine ...jacket
Silver Cloud...jacket
Columbia...jacket

/

www.ingramcontent.com/pod-product-compliance
Lightning Source LLC
Chambersburg PA
CBHW070415190526
45169CB00003B/1265